Mountain Goats

*written and photographed
by Frank Staub*

Lerner Publications Company • Minneapolis, Minnesota

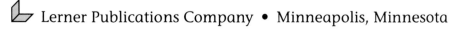

For Cindy and all those who love the
places where wild goats roam

The photographs in this book were taken in Glacier National
Park in Montana; Olympic National Park in Washington; Pike
National Forest, San Juan National Forest, and San Isabel
National Forest, all in Colorado.

Thanks to our series consultant, Sharyn Fenwick, elementary
science/math specialist. Mrs. Fenwick was the winner of the
National Science Teachers Association 1991 Distinguished
Teaching Award. She also was the recipient of the Presidential
Award for Excellence in Math and Science Teaching, representing
the state of Minnesota at the elementary level in 1992.
Special thanks to our young helpers Sam Kelley and Ben
Liestman.

Early Bird Nature Books were conceptualized by Ruth
Berman and designed by Steve Foley. Series editor is
Joelle Goldman.

Website address: www.lernerbooks.com

Library of Congress Cataloging-in-Publication Data

Staub, Frank J.
    Mountain goats / by Frank Staub.
      p.   cm. — (Early bird nature books)
    Includes index.
    ISBN 0-8225-3000-7
    1. Rocky Mountain goat—Juvenile literature. [1. Rocky
    Mountain goat.] I. Title. II. Series.
    QL737.U53S695 1994
    599.73'58—dc20   93-32491

Manufactured in the United States of America
2 3 4 5 6 7 – I/SP – 03 02 01 00 99 98

Contents

Mountain goats
live in the
United States
and Canada.
The red areas
show exactly
where mountain
goats can be found.

Be a Word Detective

Can you find these words as you read about the mountain goat's life? Be a detective and try to figure out what they mean. You can turn to the glossary on page 47 for help.

avalanches	**guard hairs**	**salt licks**
band	**kids**	**shed**
billies	**nannies**	**tree line**
bleating	**rank**	

Chapter 1

Temperatures may drop far below freezing in these mountains. What kind of animal would be able to raise a family here?

The Mountain Goat's Neighborhood

High in the mountains, the weather can be terrible. Enough snow may fall to cover a log cabin. And the wind can knock you off your feet. Even in the summer, the ground has ice in it. Only one large animal lives high in the mountains all year long. That animal is the mountain goat.

The mountain goat's scientific name is Oreamnos americanus.

Mountain goats are found in western North America. Their home is always at or above tree line, which is the highest place where trees grow. The winters are so long and cold above tree line that there are no trees at all.

Mountain goats live in the mountains of western United States and Canada.

Mountain goats can walk on rocky land because the two toes on their feet can spread apart and grip the rocks.

Most of the mountain goat's home is rocky and very steep. One false step can mean a broken leg, or even death. But mountain goats hardly ever fall because they have a good sense of balance. Their wide feet grip the rock firmly. And their thin bodies fit on narrow ledges.

Mountain goats are good climbers. They are very careful. But some dangers come without warning. Falling rocks may surprise them. And snow sliding down a mountain kills some mountain goats each year. These snow slides are called avalanches (AV-ah-lan-chez).

How do you think this mountain goat broke its horn?

Chapter 2

Mountain goats seem to like the cold and snow. What do you think keeps them warm and dry?

Living in the Cold

Winter comes early to mountain goat country. New snow may start to fall in September. But mountain goats don't have to worry about the cold. During the winter, two layers of fur keep them warm. The fur close to their bodies is like the soft wool of a sheep.

You can see the long, thick guard hairs on the mother mountain goat.

Long, thick hairs cover the woolly fur. These hairs are called guard hairs. They keep out the wind, rain, and snow.

Finding food during the winter is hard for most mountain goats. Grasses and wildflowers are a mountain goat's favorite foods. But they get buried under the snow. Luckily, mountain goats aren't picky eaters. They can chew and swallow almost anything they find. They even eat the needles of pine trees!

Sometimes it's hard for mountain goats to find enough to eat.

By late spring, most of the snow has melted. Mountain goats start to shed their winter coats. The thick fur comes off in chunks, making the goats look shaggy. Mountain goats rub against bushes to help them shed. The bushes soon become full of fluffy balls of white fur.

The winter coat on this mountain goat's head and neck has already been shed.

Mountain goats rub against bushes to help them shed (top). Fluffy balls of winter fur decorate the bushes (left).

15

Mountain goats love to lick salt.

Like most wild animals, mountain goats need salt. They don't get enough salt from the plants they eat. But in some places, the ground is full of salt. Places with lots of salt are called salt licks because animals go there to lick the salty ground. No one knows for sure why mountain goats love salt so much.

Sometimes, mountain goats climb steep and dangerous land to get salt from the ground.

Chapter 3

Mountain goats weigh 120 to 225 pounds and can grow to be about 4 feet tall at the shoulders. Why do you think mountain goats have such big shoulders?

Mountain Goat Families

Mountain goats are about the same size and shape as the goats you see on a farm. Male goats are called billies, females are called nannies, and baby goats are called kids.

It's hard to tell the difference between a male and a female mountain goat.

Nannies and billies look almost the same. They both have black horns that are 7 to 10 inches long. Big, powerful shoulders help billies and nannies climb and paw through the snow to find food. As nannies and billies grow older, their chin hairs hang down like a beard. One difference between billies and nannies is that billies spend a lot of time alone. Nannies live in small groups with the youngsters.

Mountain goats live together in groups called bands.

A group of mountain goats is called a band. Nannies, kids, and young goats live together in bands. Each band has from 2 to 20 goats. The exact number is always changing because some goats leave the band and others join. Sometimes billies form bands of their own.

The mountain goat on the right is chasing a kid who has a lower rank in the band.

Each mountain goat in a band has a rank. Those with higher ranks get the best sleeping spots and use the salt licks first. Usually, bigger nanny goats rank higher than smaller nannies. A kid has the same rank as its mother. Small goats who are one or two years old have lower ranks. But if a billy goat happens to be around, he has the lowest rank of all.

The mountain goat on the right is stepping away from a higher ranking goat.

Chapter 4

A kid usually has no brothers or sisters. When do you think kids are usually born?

Being a Kid

Mountain goats don't have many kids. Each year, only about half the nannies in a band give birth. Usually, each nanny has just one kid at a time. But sometimes twins are born. Nannies give birth in the spring when there is plenty to eat and the weather isn't too cold.

Kids are born in the spring.

By the time kids are one day old, they can run, jump, and maybe even climb.

A kid is nursing.

Kids grow quickly. They can stand up and walk right after they are born. Some kids try to climb when they are just one day old! Their first taste of food comes from nursing, or drinking their mother's milk. But when kids are two days old, they can eat plants. When they are about one month old, kids stop nursing and eat only plants.

Nannies take good care of their kids. They protect their kids from other animals. They watch their kids as they learn to climb. Nannies teach their kids almost everything they need to know about staying alive in the mountains.

Two kids from the same band get to know each other.

Kids play by pushing and wrestling.
Playing makes them strong. And playing
teaches kids how to take care of themselves. But
as their horns grow, kids touch each other less
and less because one might get stabbed.

30

Kids at play

Chapter 5

Kids stay close to their mother for one year. After one year, do you think they leave their mother for good?

Growing Up

Most young mountain goats leave their mother when they are almost one year old. But they may stay in the same band with their mother. The young goats keep growing until they are three or four. Then they are ready to have kids of their own.

Many young goats die during their first winter. Sometimes they get caught in an avalanche. But they usually die because they can't get enough to eat.

This mountain goat has lived through the winter.

Even when mountain goats do grow up, they don't live very long. By the time they are 11 years old, their teeth may be worn down. Some old mountain goats starve to death because they can't chew their food.

A mountain goat's teeth wear down from eating. Notice the nanny's flat teeth.

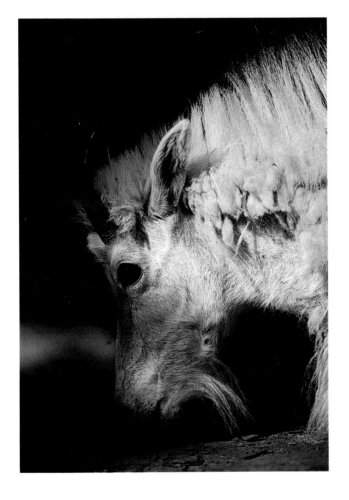

Notice the rings on this mountain goat's horn. About how old do you think it is?

You can tell how old a mountain goat is by counting the number of rings on one of its horns. A mountain goat who is two years old has one ring. When the goat is three years old, it has two rings. By its fourth birthday, it has three rings on its horn, and so on.

Chapter 6

Mountain goats are talking to each other with their bodies. Do mountain goats talk with voices too?

Mountain Goat Talk

Mountain goats sometimes make noises like grunts, hums, and snorts. Nannies and kids call to each other by bleating loudly. But mountain goats talk to each other mainly with their bodies.

A goat running or leaping toward another goat is saying, "Get out of my way!" The other goat might stand sideways and stick out its horns. In mountain goat language that means, "I don't want to fight, but I don't want to move either." In time, one goat gets scared and moves. Mountain goats "talk" to each other like this all day long. But actual fights between mountain goats almost never happen.

The goat on the right doesn't want to fight or get out of the way.

Chapter 7

Mountain lions sometimes eat mountain goats. Why don't more animals eat mountain goats?

Enemies

Mountain goats do not have many enemies. Some people hunt them. Once in a while, golden eagles catch and eat kids. And sometimes mountain lions climb above tree line

Steep, rocky land helps keep mountain goats safe from their enemies.

to look for their meals. But even with these enemies, mountain goats have little to fear. Not many animals can chase a mountain goat up a steep cliff. Mountain goats are safe from most of their enemies because they live on steep and rocky land.

Some people enjoy hunting mountain goats. But for many years, people couldn't reach the goats' home. Today, roads lead into the mountains, so we can simply drive there.

Now more people can get to places where mountain goats live.

Some people were afraid all the mountain goats would be killed off. Then people passed hunting laws. Now only a few mountain goats are shot each year.

Glacier National Park, in Montana, is one
of the best places to see mountain goats. The
cliffs have many ledges where the goats can

find grasses and wildflowers to eat. The ledges are safe places to rest, too. Maybe mountain goats even enjoy the view.

On Sharing a Book

As you know, adults greatly influence a child's attitude toward reading. When a child sees you read, or when you share a book with a child, you're sending a message that reading is important. Show the child that reading a book together is important to you. Find a comfortable, quiet place. Turn off the television and limit other distractions, such as telephone calls.

Be prepared to start slowly. Take turns reading parts of this book. Stop and talk about what you're reading. Talk about the photographs. You may find that much of the shared time is spent discussing just a few pages. This discussion time is valuable for both of you, so don't move through the book too quickly. If the child begins to lose interest, stop reading. Continue sharing the book at another time. When you do pick up the book again, be sure to revisit the parts you have already read. Most importantly, enjoy the book!

Be a Vocabulary Detective

You will find a word list on page 5. Words selected for this list are important to the understanding of the topic of this book. Encourage the child to be a word detective and search for the words as you read the book together. Talk about what the words mean and how they are used in the sentence. Do any of these words have more than one meaning? You will find these words defined in a glossary on page 47.

What about Questions?

Use questions to make sure the child understands the information in this book. Here are some suggestions:

> What did this paragraph tell us? What does this picture show? What do you think we'll learn about next? Tell me about the mountain goat's neighborhood. How is it like yours? How is it different? Could a mountain goat live in your backyard? Why/Why not? Why are there no trees found above tree line? Do other plants grow above tree line? What does a mountain goat's rank in a band mean? Which goats are part of a band? Which goats usually are not part of a band? How is a mountain goat band like your family and how is it different? What is your favorite part of the book? Why?

If the child has questions, don't hesitate to respond with questions of your own such as: What do *you* think? Why? What is it that you don't know? If the child can't remember certain facts, turn to the index.

Introducing the Index

The index is an important learning tool. It helps readers get information quickly without searching throughout the whole book. Turn to the index on page 48. Choose an entry, such as *horns,* and ask the child to use the index to find out how long a mountain goat's horns are. Repeat this exercise with as many entries as you like. Ask the child to point out the differences between an index and a glossary. (The index helps readers find information quickly, while the glossary tells readers what words mean.)

Where in the World?

Many plants and animals found in Early Bird Nature Books series live in parts of the world other than the United States. Encourage the child to find the places mentioned in this book on a world map or globe. Take time to talk about climate, terrain, and how you might live in such places.

All the World in Metric

Although our monetary system is in metric units (based on multiples of 10), the United States is one of the few countries in the world that does not use the metric system of measurement. Here are some conversion activities you and the child can do using a calculator:

WHEN YOU KNOW:	MULTIPLY BY:	TO FIND:
miles	1.609	kilometers
feet	0.3048	meters
inches	2.54	centimeters
gallons	3.787	liters
tons	0.907	metric tons
pounds	0.454	kilograms

Activities

Make up a story about mountain goats. Be sure to include information from this book. Draw or paint pictures to illustrate the story.

Go to a hilly area to experience walking up and down steep slopes. Walk on hands and feet, so you're walking more like a mountain goat. What do you think it's like for mountain goats?

Visit a farm or zoo to see, hear, and smell goats. Are they like mountain goats?

Visit a natural history museum to see displays of mountain goats.

Glossary

avalanches (AV-ah-lan-chez)—large amounts of snow sliding quickly and powerfully down mountains

band—a group of 2 to 20 mountain goats

billies—male mountain goats. One male mountain goat is called a billy.

bleating—making the sound of a goat

guard hairs—long, thick hairs that grow over a mountain goat's soft underfur. Guard hairs keep mountain goats dry and warm.

kids—baby mountain goats

nannies—female mountain goats. One female mountain goat is called a nanny.

rank—a position of importance within a group (band)

salt licks—places where mountain goats lick salt that comes from the ground

shed—to lose an old coat of fur

tree line—the highest place on a mountain where trees grow

47

Index